ISBN 978-1-5280-9663-8
PIBN 11013120

Wheat

STA/STA

OUTLOOK & SITUATION

Table 1.--Wheat: Supply, disappearance, area, and prices, marketing years 1980-83*

	Million bushels			
Supply				
Beginning stocks, June 1	902	989	1,164	1,550
Production	2,374	2,799	2,809	2,353 + 180
Imports 1/	3	3	7	3
Total	3,279	3,791	3,980	3,906 + 180
Domestic disappearance				
Food	611	600	610	620 + 5
Seed	114	112	95	90 + 5
Feed 2/	51	142	200	250 + 75
Total	776	854	905	960 + 80
Exports 1/	1,514	1,773	1,525	1,400 + 150
Total disappearance	2,290	2,627	2,430	2,360 + 175
Ending stocks, May 31	989	1,164	1,550	1,546 + 175
	Million acres			
Area				
Planted	80.6	88.9	87.3	
Harvested	71.0	81.0	78.8	
Set-aside and diverted	--	--	5.8	
Allotment/Nat'l program	75.0	84.5	--	
	Bushels per acre			
Yield per harvested acre	33.4	34.5	35.6	
	Dollars per bushel			
Prices				
Received by farmers	3.91	3.65	3.53	3.50-3.75
Loan rate	3.00	3.20	3.55	3.65
Target rate	3.63	3.81	4.05	4.30

1/ Imports and exports include flour and other products expressed in wheat equivalent. 2/ Residual, approximates feed use and includes negligible quantities used
for alcoholic beverages.

* Totals may not add due to rounding.

National Economics Division
Economics Research Service
U.S. Department of Agriculture
Washington, D.C. 20250

The Wheat *Outlook and Situation* is published in February, May, August, and November. Approved by the World Agricultural Outlook Board and summary released May 12, 1983.

The next summary of the *Wheat Outlook and Situation* is scheduled for release on July 26. It will appear on the AGNET computer system by 3:30 ET the same day. The full text and tabular materials will be added to AGNET approximately 2 business days later. For more information on AGNET, call (402) 472-1892.

Contributors
Domestic
Allen Schienbein-Analyst
Alberta Smith-Statistics
(202) 447-8444

World
Bradley Karmen
(202) 447-8879

Summary

Heavy Program Participation
Will Cut 1983 U.S. Wheat Crop

Harvesting of the 1983 wheat crop is underway, with growers expected to combine the smallest acreage in 4 years, a result of Government efforts to reduce U.S. wheat supplies. Wheat production has ballooned to record heights in each of the last three harvests, burdening the industry with excessively large stocks.

Initially, winter wheat seeding was down 3.4 million acres from 1982/83, but enrollment in the payment-in-kind (PIK) program, announced after planting, idled additional cropland, leaving an expected 47 million acres to be harvested, 11 million less than last year. Higher yields will offset some of the acreage reduction, but as of May 1, 1983, winter wheat production was forecast at 1.9 billion bushels, 215 million below 1982's record. In addition, heavy program participation by spring wheat growers will decrease their 1983 plantings about a third, which will mean a sharp cutback from last year's record crop of 700 million bushels. The total 1983 wheat crop is forecast at 2.35 billion, down 450 million from 1982's record.

Despite the reduced harvest, total supply will be only fractionally smaller than 1982/83's record because of a large carryin. Early prospects for demand are limited, with exports expected to be down from 1982/83 and only a slight increase in domestic use. Because total wheat use will about match 1983's production, yearend stocks on May 31, 1984, will remain record high. However, "free" readily marketable stocks will increase substantially because nearly half of the stocks isolated in the farmer-owned reserve will be used for PIK. Under these conditions, the average farm price may be only slightly better than 1982/83's $3.53 a bushel, within a range from $3.50 to $3.75.

The largest wheat supply on record dominated 1982/83. Concurrently, the volume of exports declined substantially from 1981/82's record pace. Domestic food and feed use of wheat rose, though not enough to prevent a stock buildup for the third straight year. The large supply and weak exports pushed farm prices below the $3.55-a-bushel loan rate for most of the season. Many eligible producers found the farmer-owned reserve an attractive marketing option and placed a fifth of 1982's production in that program.

Early prospects for world wheat output in 1983/84 suggest that production may be close to 1982/83's record 479 million metric tons. With large carryin stocks, the supplies of major exporters will be more than adequate to meet import demand, even if their production falls slightly. World trade will probably be below the 100-million-ton mark, with aggressive competition among exporters likely to continue.

Wheat Situation

OUTLOOK FOR 1983/84

Reduced Harvested Area Cuts
1983 Winter Crop Substantially

Faced with serious and worsening surpluses of wheat supplies, USDA added the payment-in-kind (PIK) program to its earlier announced 15-percent acreage reduction (ARP) and 5-percent paid land diversion (PLD) programs. In exchange for idling a large portion of their cropland, producers who participate in PIK, will receive as compensation wheat stocks owned by the Commodity Credit Corporation (CCC) or obligated to the regular or reserve loan programs. Farmers signed up to include 86 percent of their 90.9 million acres of wheat cropland base in the overall reduction program, designating 59 percent of their enrollment to the partial and whole-base PIK. If all participants remain in compliance (those in the ARP and PLD may withdraw without a penalty), 32 million acres of wheat land may never see a combine this year.

Last fall winter wheat seedings were only about 3.5 million acres below the area that produced the record 1982 crop. This was an indication that the ARP and PLD programs would be of limited effectiveness in lowering 1983 production. However, because price expectations were disappointing, producers responded favorably to the PIK option. Nearly 21 million acres of the winter wheat base will be idled this year, leading to an expected harvested acreage of 47 million, 11 million below last year. With record high yields offsetting some of the effect of reduced acreage, the May 1 forecast of the 1983 winter wheat crop is 1.9 billion bushels—more than 200 million below 1982's record. The section on wheat by class gives more breakdown on the production forecast.

Heavy Program Participation
To Sharply Reduce Spring Wheat Crop

Prospects for excessively large spring wheat supplies and the lowest prices in 4 years heavily influenced producers of Durum, Hard Red Spring, and White Spring wheat to enroll nearly all of the base acreage possible in the 1983 acreage reduction programs. As a result, an estimated 7 million acres of wheat land, mostly in the Northern Plains, will not be seeded in 1983. While seeding may be delayed because of extended cold, wet weather, good soil moisture should be favorable to yields. Still, because of program compliance, total production could be below the drought-stricken 1980 crop of 479 million bushels.

1983 Harvest To Be Lowest in 4 Years;
Supplies To Remain Large

An exceptionally mild winter and near-optimal precipitation over the last few months has reduced the uncertainty that often surrounds the early-season crop outlook. Many areas in the Great Plains have the potential for record yields. However, excessive rains, particularly in the South, have reduced yield potential in some

Soft Red Winter States. Overall, the large acreage reduction due to program compliance is the major factor that will reduce the total 1983 wheat harvest to a projected 2.35 billion bushels, about 15 percent below last year's record 2.8 billion. Since winter wheat accounts for the bulk of the crop, the uncertainty surrounding the current forecast is relatively small. Chances are about 2 out of 3 that the final outcome will fall within 180 million bushels of the current projection. Even with the expected drop in production, 1983/84 will have total supplies near 1982/83's alltime high because of record carryover stocks.

This year's effort to bring wheat supply and use into balance depends much more heavily on the acreage reduction programs than demand expansion. Current projections for 1983/84 disappearance indicate a modest decline from last season. The potential for another large global harvest in 1983, including gains in major importing countries, underlines the forecast for a slight decrease in world wheat trade in 1983/84. Thus, market competition among major exporters will remain keen, with U.S. exports likely to decline nearly one-tenth in 1983/84.

Domestic use of wheat for feed may exceed 1982/83's projected 200 million bushels, as tightening feed grain supplies will likely make wheat more price competitive through the early months of the season. Food use is projected to increase in line with the past growth trend. In total, 1983/84 wheat disappearance could about match production, so yearend stocks will likely remain record high, well above levels of recent years.

One important aspect is that "free" or readily marketable stocks will increase substantially, because nearly half of the farmer-owned reserve (FOR) will be used for PIK. Also, except for the 147-million-bushel Food Security Reserve, all stocks belonging to the CCC will find their way into the market. Furthermore, early entry of grain into the FOR will not be allowed, contrasting the immediate entry policy in 1982/83. For 1983/84, the FOR loan rate was established at the $3.65 loan rate, compared with $4 in 1982/83. So, the incentive to isolate the 1983 crop from the market will be smaller.

These supply/demand prospects suggest that the farm price for wheat next year could average only marginally above this year's $3.53, with a range of $3.50 to $3.75 a bushel. Heavy participation in Government programs will make a good share of 1983's crop eligible for the $3.65 loan. Still, market prices could be at or slightly below the loan rate at harvest time because PIK grain from currently unmarketable reserve stocks becomes available at that time. However, the program feature whereby the CCC will pay up to 5 months of storage costs on PIK grain should allow orderly marketing thereby softening the price-depressing effect. Currently outstanding wheat export sales for delivery in 1983/84 are nearly 55 percent behind the pace of a year ago. If this continues, it will also likely limit any early-season price advances.

U. S. Wheat Exports by Months, Marketing Years 1981/82 and 1982/83

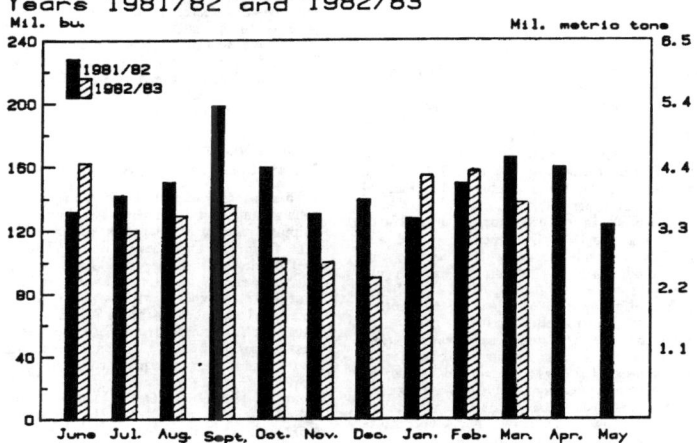

Includes flour and products in wheat equivalent.

Wheat Prices Received by Farmers

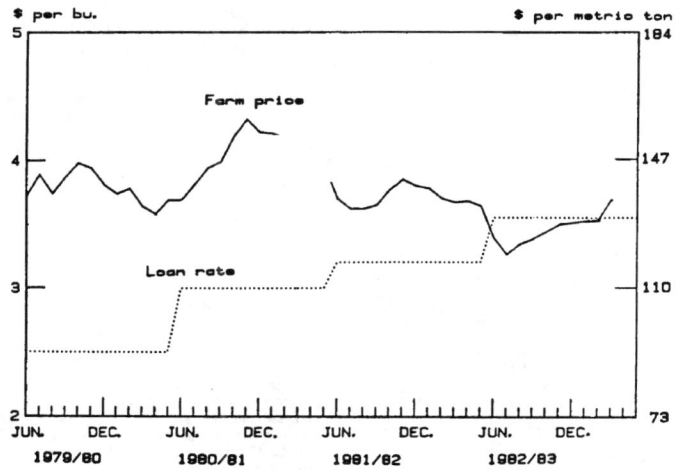

THE CURRENT SITUATION

Wheat Stocks at Record High; Disappearance Fades

Wheat stocks on April 1 totaled a record 1.9 billion bushels, 20 percent more than a year ago. This is enough wheat to sustain domestic consumption for about 2 years without any added production. Since last June, producers placed one-fifth of 1982's record production into the reserve. Adding this to FOR stocks from prior crops, total wheat in the reserve represented 58 percent of April's supply. These stocks, plus another 185 million bushels owned by CCC, are not available to commercial buyers at current market prices.

A 14-percent decline in exports during June-March offset the tightening supplies. Only domestic food and feed use will show expanded consumption during this crop year, while seed use and, particularly, exports will decline. The pace of wheat use during April and May is not expected to change appreciably, leading to another buildup of yearend stocks—the third year in a row.

Domestic food use during June-March was running about 1.5 percent above a year earlier. Production of wheat flour in calendar 1982 was the second largest on record, up slightly from a year ago (table 3A). However, overseas flour shipments rose during this time, so the net effect was reduced domestic flour use. On a per capita basis, domestic flour consumption in 1982 dropped 2 pounds. This blip in a rather stable series for food use may be a result of the recession, which may have reduced away-from-home food expenditures, thereby resulting in lower consumption of bakery products.

Wheat: supply and disappearance

Item	June-March	
	1981/82	1982/83
	Million bushels	
June 1 stocks	989	1,164
Production	2,799	2,809
Total supply 1/	3,790	3,980
Exports	1,490	1,288
Food	513	519
Seed	84	79
Feed	146	225
Total disappearance	2,233	2,111
April 1 stocks	1,557	1,869

1/ Includes imports.

The pace of wheat feeding during June-March was slightly above the annual projection of 200 million bushels. According to the method used to quantify feeding—the residual between stocks at one date compared with the estimated stocks at a later date—feeding was about 80 million bushels more than a year earlier. This indicates increased wheat use in feed rations. Low Soft Red Winter wheat prices all season likely meant more wheat in poultry rations. The situation was similar for hard wheats in livestock feed.

January-March Exports Improve; Season Shipments To Be Lower

This season's export loadings of wheat continue to be substantially off from the 1981/82 record. The monthly shipping rate during January-March increased 25 percent from the slow tempo established during the first half of the marketing year (June-December). However, with the end of the season nearly at hand, it is obvious that 1982/83 exports will be nearly 250 million bushels short of last year's record 1.77 billion bushels. Much of this shortfall comes from noticeable reductions in purchases from the Soviet Union, China, and both Western and Eastern Europe. In addition, some traditional Latin American customers cut back on buying because of financial restraints. Only sales to India and Iraq were substantially larger. Total U.S. exports this season, at 1.525 billion bushels, will still be the second largest on record, but the decrease from last season will end the run of 5 successive years of increasing volumes.

Farm Price Shows Some Seasonal Improvement

Monthly average farm prices during the first half of 1982/83 were in the doldrums, being unable to top the $3.55-a-bushel loan rate. This barrier was finally overcome as increased export demand, coupled with record placements of the 1982 crop into the reserve, and the announcement of the PIK program in early January pushed the average price up to $3.65 a bushel during the first 4 months of 1983. Still, it is likely that the 1982/83 farm price will average below the loan rate, a situation that last occurred in 1968/69.

Currently, the leading question concerns the level of farm prices for the new crop. As of early May, July contract prices in the three futures markets were fairly close to quotations of a year ago. This could be interpreted as signaling new-crop prices similiar to those in 1982. Since the 1983/84 loan rate was raised 10 cents a bushel to $3.65, farm prices may again be below the loan rate during the coming harvest. Any major price increase during 1983/84 will hinge on unforeseen events here and abroad that would improve world trade prospects.

WORLD WHEAT OUTLOOK

Production Prospects for 1983/84

Winter grain acreage sown in the Northern Hemisphere last fall was down slightly, mainly reflecting the United States' major effort to cut production. It appears that other areas will continue their efforts to expand production for domestic needs, and exporters will attempt to further augment their markets. Taking the widespread moderate winter into consideration, and assuming normal spring wheat growing conditions, the 1983/84 global wheat harvest could be close to last year's. record outturn of 479 million metric tons.

The area sown to winter wheat is estimated to be up slightly in *Western Europe*, and the condition of the crop seems to be unusually good as the spring growing season develops. The dry conditions on the Iberian Peninsula will affect the size of that area's production. Fall seeding of wheat in *Eastern Europe* increased slightly in all countries except Poland, where early-season dryness caused poor stand development. Some spring replanting is likely, but Poland's harvest may suffer from the scarcity of yield-boosting inputs—fertilizer and pesticides. Area may be down in the *Soviet Union*, because dry fall weather persisted at seeding time causing some traditional wheat land to be left unplanted. However, a mild winter followed by spring rains was beneficial to both winter and spring wheat prospects. Although uncertainty surrounds the final USSR wheat outturn, with much depending on the development of the spring wheat crop, 1983's production is likely to be up slightly from 1982.

In *North Africa*, Algeria, Tunisia, and Morocco intended to expand their wheat growing area. However, early-season dryness delayed seeding and may have prevented some area from being sown. Favorable conditions have returned to some parts of North Africa, but production seems likely to fall below last year. Reflecting a shift from rapeseed production, a 3 to 4-percent increase in winter wheat planting in *China* could mean larger production if favorable moisture continues. Continued expansion in *India's* wheat area is likely to push 1983 production above the 1982 record. Excellent development conditions should produce enough wheat in *Pakistan* to continue its recent exporting of surpluses.

Despite lower initial payments by the Wheat Board, *Canadian* growers intend to plant nearly 7 percent more area than that which produced the 1982 record crop. Favorable spring weather will likely make these intentions a reality. Flood damage will probably make *Mexico's* wheat harvest lower than in 1982. In the *Southern Hemisphere*, early planting projections are down sharply in Brazil, but only slightly in Argentina, whereas record seedings are forecast for Australia.

World Wheat Trade
May Be Down Slightly

On balance, the world wheat situation in 1983/84 will most likely resemble the previous year: production will exceed use; world trade will be slightly below the 100-million-ton mark; and prices are unlikely to rise significantly from 1982/83. Because of large carryin stocks, exporters' supplies will be more than adequate to meet import requirements in 1983/84, even where production falls slightly. Aggressive competition among exporters is likely to continue, as each seeks to maintain a share of the contracting world market. As a result, the United States—the largest exporter—will probably see a significant decline in export volume, falling more than 20 percent below the record shipments in 1981/82.

World wheat supply and distribution, 1978-83 1/

Marketing year	Beginning stocks 2/	Production	Total exports	Total utilization 3/
	Million metric tons			
1978/79	84.3	446.8	72.0	430.2
1979/80	100.9	423.3	86.0	443.8
1980/81	80.4	441.5	94.2	446.6
1981/82	75.3	448.6	102.2	440.8
1982/83 4/	83.1	479.3	100.2	465.6
1983/84 5/	96.7	477.8	97.4	462.4

1/Data in this table are based on an aggregate of differing local marketing years and will, therefore, differ from July-June data appearing elsewhere in this report. 2/Stocks data are only for selected countries and exclude such important countries as the USSR, China, and part of Eastern Europe for which stocks data are not available; the aggregate stocks levels have, however, been adjusted for estimated year-to-year changes in USSR grain stocks. 3/For countries for which stock data are not available, or for which no adjustments have been made for year-to-year changes, utilization estimates assume a constant stock level. 4/Preliminary. 5/Projected.

Source: Foreign Agricultural Service, World Grain Situation.

STRATEGIES OF THE MAJOR WHEAT EXPORTERS

The major wheat exporters—the United States, Canada, Argentina, the EC, and Australia—have resorted to more aggressive export marketing this season because of mounting pressures from record world production, huge stocks, low prices, and stagnant trade. Of the major exporters, only Australia had a smaller wheat crop in 1982/83—output was 47 percent below that of 1981/82. Export programs—ranging from traditional ones, such as donations, barter, credit guarantees, and supply agreements, to the more controversial ones, such as subsidies, price concessions, and low-interest financing—have been used extensively during the past year.

The world trade situation is complex from the perspective of both the exporters and importers. While export prices for wheat are the lowest in several years, many importers have been unable to increase purchases because of financial constraints. The major cause of the depressed prices is a high global stocks-to-use ratio due mainly to above-trend world production. This ratio will reach 21 percent by the end of 1982/83, the highest since the late 1970's, and it is likely to remain near this level for at least another year.

After growing about 6 percent a year during the 1970's, world wheat trade in 1983/84 will likely fall below 100 million tons for the first time in 3 years. This will cause major exporters to seek new ways to dispose of their growing exportable supplies. Tables A and B compare exports, ending stocks, and the market shares of each of the major wheat exporters during the last two decades.

During the 1970's, the United States increased its share of exports the most because it was the only exporter able to increase production fast enough to support the growing needs of importers. At the same time, though, import demand grew so fast that other exporters were also able to increase their export volume even though their market shares declined. Australia, Argentina, and France generally move their surplus production into export markets, keeping carryover stocks very small. When trade leveled off, such as in the last 2 years, Canada and the United States adjusted by holding stocks. The farmer-owned reserve program provides incentives for U.S. growers to isolate wheat from the market. This was especially true in 1982/83 when nearly a fifth of production went into the reserve. Relative to production, Canada and the United States hold the largest stocks. However, Canadian stocks have declined sharply from the high levels of the early 1970's.

Major exporters have tried to assure themselves of some degree of trade stability through various export arrangements. Current wheat export arrangements used by each country are indicated by a Y in the following table:

Export Arrangements

	Long-term agreements	Extended payments	Credit guarantees	Below-market interest rates and price discounts
United States	Y	Y	Y	Y
Canada	Y	Y	Y	Y
Australia	Y	Y		
France*	Y		Y	Y
Argentina	Y			Y

* Major EC exporter

Australia

The Australian Wheat Board (AWB) is the sole marketing authority for its domestic and export sales. Because Australia has little storage capacity, only pipeline supplies are held at the end of the marketing year. The Government does not provide credit guarantees for export sales. The AWB does provide extended payment terms, but only to a limited number of overseas markets. Traditionally, China and Egypt have been the recipients. Besides these countries, Australia has supply agreements with Japan, Iraq, and Iran. These agreements account for roughly 5 million tons.

Argentina

Argentine export sales are transacted by the National Grain Board and private companies. Argentina, the smallest major wheat exporter, engages in long-term agreements to move supplies into the export market. Such agreements with China, Iran, Algeria, and Iraq account for nearly half of its exports. Several countries—Chile, Peru, Haiti, Brazil, Bolivia, and Czechoslovakia—made commitments for the purchase of 1982 wheat and will probably buy from Argentina in 1983, even though there are no formal agreements. Most of Argentina's wheat exports are shipped within the first half of its marketing year to make room for the export seasons of coarse grains and soybeans. Argentina sold most of this year's extraordinarily large crop by undercutting the U.S. export price by as much as $25 a ton. Wheat stocks are kept at a minimum because of storage and financial constraints. The Government does not provide credit to importers.

Canada

Canada is the second largest wheat trader, accounting for nearly one-fifth of world exports. Like its Australian counterpart, the Canadian Wheat Board (CWB) is the sole legal exporter. Canada has agreements with the USSR, China, Brazil, Algeria, Japan, East Germany, Cuba, Jamaica, Lebanon, Ghana, and Iraq. These agreements account for 12 to 15 million tons, or two-thirds of Canada's total exports.

Canada also offers credit to importers. The Government provides guarantees to the CWB to extend credit to certain countries. The CWB provides credit by borrowing from banks for up to 3 years at interest rates 4 percent below prime. In the past, credit sales totaled 3 to 4 million tons. For 1982, the Government approved credit guarantees to the USSR for up to C$1 billion of grain sales and to East Germany. In recent years, Canada has also provided credit to Poland, China, Brazil, Haiti, Jamaica, and Israel. Long-term credit—over 3 years—is also available, but no shipments have been made under this program for years.

France

France has dramatically increased its share of the export market in this and each of the three prior seasons by using the export subsidies it receives as a member of the European Community and by using export credits guaranteed by the France Export Guaranty

Agency (COFACE). The EC adjusts the export subsidy to reflect the difference between the world price and its high domestic price, depending upon how much wheat it wishes to move into the export market. Current export subsidies are $67 a ton, but they were higher earlier in the year, when world prices were lower. The early May Rotterdam world price is $200.

France has supply or credit arrangements with the USSR, China, Cuba, Brazil, Algeria, Egypt, Morocco, Portugal, Poland, and Vietnam. Credit arrangements are for a maximum of 2 years at market interest rates. However, below-market interest rates were recently offered to Morocco.

United States

The United States uses various programs to promote its wheat exports, ranging from the P.L. 480 program initiated in 1954 to the newest blended credit program. The United States has bilateral agreements with the USSR and China for a combined minimum of about 7 million tons of wheat.

P.L. 480 provides for concessional sales to developing countries with repayment terms as long as 40 years and extremely low interest rates. About 3.5 million tons were shipped under this program last year.

USDA also guarantees credit through the General Sales Manager (GSM)-102 program run by the Commodity Credit Corporation (CCC). Credit is for up to 3 years at commercial rates. The Government guarantees 98 percent of the principal at up to 8 percent interest. In fiscal 1982, GSM-102 sales guarantees were used for 3.72 million tons of wheat exports.

In fiscal 1983, $1.75 billion was allocated for a blended credit program for all agricultural exports. Out of this, $350 million will be used for interest-free, direct government export credit under GSM-5 legislation and will be combined with the remaining $1.4 million in guarantees to achieve an interest rate 20 percent less than market rates. As of late April, about $525 million worth of wheat sales have been financed this way, but only about $1 billion of the $1.75 billion has been allocated to date. Under a separate program, the United States sold 1 million tons of wheat flour to Egypt at a price considerably below the U.S. export price. The U.S. Government will subsidize the price difference by providing additional wheat out of Government inventory to the millers.

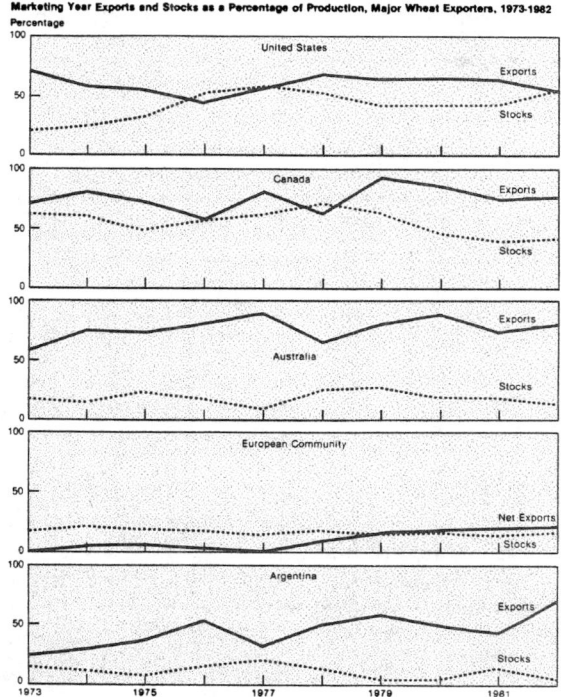

Marketing Year Exports and Stocks as a Percentage of Production, Major Wheat Exporters, 1973-1982

Table A.--World wheat exports (July/June, excluding intra-EC)

Exporters	1960-64 average	1965-69 average	1970-74 average	1975-79 average	1980/81	1981/82	1982/83 (prel.)	1983/84 (forecast)
				Million metric tons				
United States	19.5	19.0	25.6	31.8	41.9	49.1	41.5	38.0
Canada	11.0	11.3	12.7	13.9	17.0	17.8	21.0	21.5
Australia	6.1	6.5	7.5	9.8	10.6	11.0	7.5	11.0
EC	3.3	4.2	4.9	7.6	14.7	15.5	15.5	15.5
Argentina	2.6	3.4	1.9	3.9	3.9	4.3	8.5	6.5
Other	5.7	8.2	7.5	5.2	6.2	4.5	6.2	4.9
Total 1/	48.2	52.6	60.2	72.2	94.2	102.2	100.2	97.4
				Percent share of exports				
United States	40.5	36.1	42.5	44.0	44.5	48.0	41.4	39.0
Canada	22.8	21.5	21.1	19.3	18.0	17.4	20.9	22.1
Australia	12.7	12.3	12.5	13.6	11.2	10.8	7.5	11.3
EC	6.8	8.0	8.1	10.5	15.6	15.2	15.5	15.9
Argentina	5.4	6.5	3.2	5.4	4.1	4.2	8.5	6.7
Other	11.8	15.6	12.5	7.2	6.6	4.4	6.2	5.0
Total 1/	100.0	100.0	100.0	100.0	100.0	100.0	100.0	100.0

1/ Total may not add because of rounding.

Table B.--World wheat ending stocks

Exporters	1960-64 average	1965-69 average	1970-74 average	1975-79 average	1980/81	1981/82	1982/83 (prel.)	1983/84 (forecast)
				Million metric tons				
United States	33.2	20.1	17.3	26.0	26.9	31.7	42.2	37.3
Canada	13.4	19.2	12.8	11.9	8.6	9.7	11.2	11.2
Australia	.9	4.0	1.9	2.9	2.1	3.0	1.1	2.7
EC	7.8	7.2	7.2	7.7	8.8	7.7	10.0	10.7
Argentina	1.4	.6	.6	1.0	.4	.7	.5	.5
Other	17.3	37.0	30.6	36.3	28.5	30.3	31.7	49.8
Total 1/	74.0	88.1	70.4	85.8	75.3	83.1	96.7	112.2
				Percent share of stocks				
United States	44.9	22.8	24.6	30.3	35.7	38.1	43.6	33.2
Canada	18.1	21.8	18.2	13.9	11.4	11.7	11.6	10.0
Australia	1.2	4.5	2.7	3.4	2.8	3.6	1.1	2.4
EC	10.5	8.2	10.2	9.0	11.7	9.3	10.3	9.5
Argentina	1.9	.7	.8	1.1	.5	.8	.5	.4
Other	23.4	42.0	43.5	42.3	37.9	36.5	32.8	44.4
Total 1/	100.0	100.0	100.0	100.0	100.0	100.0	100.0	100.0

1/ Total may not add because of rounding.

WHEAT BY CLASS

Program Compliance Reduces
1983 HRW Crop

Prospects for the 1983 Hard Red Winter (HRW) wheat crop have been up and down. Without being aware that PIK would come along, HRW growers seeded nearly as much acreage last fall as that which produced the record 1982 crop. While dryness threatened early development, a relatively mild Great Plains winter and improved precipitation brightened prospects. At the same time that prospects were improving, growers were faced with decisions about enrolling in the PIK acreage reduction program, and enrollment was surprisingly high. So, based on conditions as of May 1, only weeks from the start of harvest, the 1983 HRW crop is forecast at 1.11 billion bushels, 11 percent short of last year's record 1.26 billion and the smallest production in three seasons.

The May estimate is still subject to last-minute harvesting decisions and weather. Wheat currently planted and growing on conservation use acreage designated for the 15-percent ARP and 5-percent PLD could be harvested if producers who enrolled decide not to comply with those programs. Those farmers in ARP and PLD who decide not to comply lose their program benefits while farmers in the PIK portion not only lose their benefits but are also subject to a monetary penalty.

The accelerated export pace since January has helped augment the disappearance of 1982/83's excessive HRW supplies. This pickup also helped to spark the only major price advance of the Kansas City market all season. Still, the estimate of 900 million bushels of HRW stocks on April 1 is 30 percent larger than the record inventory last April. FOR and CCC stocks represent a much larger share of the April supply—70 percent, compared with 55 percent in 1982.

1982/83 HRS Export Season Looks Bright;
Sharp Reduction in 1983 Crop Likely

One of the few bright spots for 1982/83 has been the strength of Hard Red Spring (HRS) exports. This is the only wheat class where exports are expected to be above last year (table 2). Loadings could nearly match the record 245 million bushels exported 10 seasons ago. While the traditional Western European desire for high-protein U.S. wheat faded somewhat, Asian and South American customers expanded purchases of HRS from the United States. Prices for this high-quality U.S. wheat were the lowest in 4 years, with the price of 14-percent protein often on par with or at a discount to HRW ordinary protein (12 percent).

Despite the relatively high prices, April 1 HRS stocks remained a record- large 510 million bushels. Nearly a third of the 1982 crop was placed into the FOR. This pushed the total HRS isolated from the market to over two-thirds of April's stocks. However, the preponderance of acreage that was enrolled into the partial and whole-base PIK programs means that a sizable share of FOR stocks will be freed up for marketing during 1983/84. Spring wheat growers are likely to withdraw a larger share of acreage from production than growers of any other class. Over 95 percent of their wheat base is enrolled in 1983 programs, suggesting HRS production between 325 to 375 million bushels, down considerably from 1982's 500- million-bushel harvest.

Durum Stocks Remain Large;
1983 Production Prospects Down

Record amounts of Durum continue to be in storage facilities throughout Northern Plains growing areas. April 1 stocks totaled 164 million bushels, a fourth greater than in 1982. With record Durum supplies pressuring the marketplace, producers found the farmer-owned reserve an important alternative to sales. A third of their 1982 production was placed into the reserve, meaning that over 100 million bushels of Durum—two-thirds of total stocks—are isolated from sales at current prices.

The large FOR stocks have done little to strengthen prices, because export demand has been particularly weak. Recent market prices have been sparked by expanded foreign sales for delivery next marketing year. However, Durum exports during 1982/83 will be around 55 million bushels, the smallest in 6 marketing years. Expanded foreign production in 1982 (including a record Canadian crop) along with large old-crop stocks, ballooned the world's Durum supply. This caused Durum prices to remain fairly steady at around $4 a bushel in Minneapolis, 10 to 15 percent below a year ago. New-crop prices will be tied to crop developments but will also be influenced by the expected heavy payoff of reserve Durum to PIK participants. Thus, the increased amount of readily marketable Durum during 1983/84 will likely limit price advances.

Because either Durum or Hard Red Spring wheat can be grown on the same acreage, the price expectation of each variety may cause some changes in final planting decisions. Thus, the Durum production estimate ranges from 80 to 100 million bushels, compared with last year's 148 million.

SRW Export Pace Declines;
Reduced 1983 Crop Likely

The decline of Soft Red Winter (SRW) exports during 1982/83 resulted in April 1 stocks of 130 million bushels, nearly 10 percent larger than a year earlier. This year's exports are off 120 million bushels from 1981/82's record 460 million. SRW has been overwhelmingly the lowest priced U.S. wheat at dockside all season; yet, foreign competition has made inroads into overseas markets. The most significant shortfall comes from a 78-million-bushel drop in Chinese purchases. Some expansion was noted from Latin American and African buyers, likely due to implementation of the blended credit export program. This season's lagging disappearance of SRW will result in abnormally large stocks; the June 1 carryover could climb to nearly 90 million bushels, the largest ever.

SRW producer enrollment in the 1983 acreage reduction programs was much smaller than for other classes. However, 1983 compliance is expected to be up substantially from 1982's level, because the acreage enrolled about doubled. Also significant to prospects for the 1983 SRW harvest is the bigger-than-expected signup in the partial and whole-base PIK programs in States accustomed to double-cropping. So, the May 1 crop forecast of 527 million bushels is 14 percent below last year's 610 million.

11

Cash Wheat Prices, 1982/83*

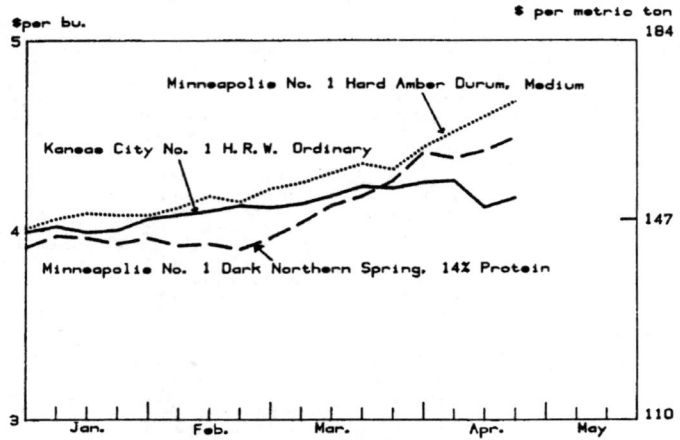

$per bu. $ per metric ton

Minneapolis No. 1 Hard Amber Durum, Medium

Kansas City No. 1 H.R.W. Ordinary

Minneapolis No. 1 Dark Northern Spring, 14% Protein

Jan.   Feb.   Mar.   Apr.   May

* Thursday Price.

Cash Wheat Prices, 1982/83*

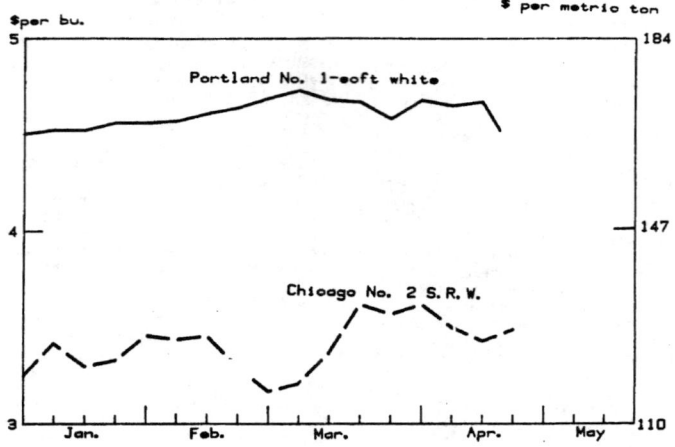

$per bu. $ per metric ton

Portland No. 1-soft white

Chicago No. 2 S.R.W.

Jan.   Feb.   Mar.   Apr.   May

*Thursday Price.

White Wheat Receives Top Prices in 1982/83; Record Yields Increase 1983 Harvest

As 1982/83 draws to a close, it is obvious that Soft White wheat will have the distinction of being the premium-priced wheat, an unusual circumstance for this low-protein wheat. The combination of a 16-percent production cutback in a crop year that saw a record harvest for all wheat, heavy placement of 1981 and the 1982 crops into the FOR, and strong producer resistance to selling at low prices helped keep farm prices of White wheat 40 to 50 cents a bushel above the national average for much of this season. The extremely short 1983 Australian wheat harvest also helped strengthen prices, as Australia is a major grower of White wheat varieties. Price strength held even though export activity, although strong, trailed last season's record pace by nearly 22 percent. Pricing for the remainder of the year will turn on new-crop prospects, particularly as to the quantity of FOR wheat that will be required to meet PIK requirements. The release of large FOR stocks onto the free market may temporarily depress prices.

Fall seeding for the 1983 White winter wheat crop was up fractionally in the Pacific Northwest. In the final analysis, over 85 percent of the base acreage was enrolled in the combined acreage reduction programs, so some acreage will be plowed under, hayed, or grazed in order to meet the 2-million-plus acres required to be in conserving use for 1983. While harvested acreage will be lower, fields are in good to excellent condition, indicating record yields in the Pacific Northwest. In turn, lower program enrollment by Eastern White wheat growers will result in more area harvested. In combination, the May 1 estimate of the 1983 White winter wheat harvest, at 255 million bushels, makes it the only class with increasing production in 1983.

Rye Imports Expand; 1983 Production May Be Up

Despite a significant dropoff of export activity, rye disappearance during June-March was still slightly above the pace of a year earlier. This was due to the largest rye imports in over 20 years. Although totaling only 2.6 million bushels, imports represented 10 percent of 1982/83's total supply. Much of this rye ended up as feed stock, but the lowest carryin in recent years caused large purchases of Canadian rye in order to meet early-season milling demand.

Planted acreage in the major producing States in the Northern Plains is up 40 percent, possibly because the 1983 acreage reduction program does not apply. Stands were in good to excellent condition going into winter dormancy, but a cool, wet spring has delayed development. Nevertheless, the 1983 rye crop could exceed last year's 20.8 million bushels.

Rye: supply and disappearance

Item	June-March	
	1981/82	1982/83
	Million bushels	
June 1 stocks	4.1	3.1
Production	18.8	20.8
Total supply 1/	23.1	26.4
Exports	1.5	0.2
Food	2.9	2.8
Seed	4.2	4.2
Industrial	1.8	2.0
Feed	6.9	9.2
Total disappearance	17.3	18.4
April 1 stocks	5.8	8.0

1/ Includes imports.

INDEX OF TABLES

NOTICE

Your subscription to this publication may be due to expire soon. If so, you will be notified by the Government Printing Office (GPO) and invited to renew. GPO will send you ONLY ONE notice, usually about 90 days before your subscription is up. To ensure uninterrupted service, return the card promptly with your renewal check. For subscription information about this or any other publication of the Economic Research Service, write: EMS Inf., Rm. 440 GHI, USDA, Washington, D.C. 20250. Or call (202) 447-8590.

Table 2.--Wheat classes: marketing year supply and disappearance 1/

Year beginning June 1	Supply			Disappearance			Ending stocks May 31
	Beginning stocks	Production	Total 2/	Domestic use	Exports	Total	
Million bushels							
1979/80:							
Hard Winter	423	1,089	1,512	347	725	1,072	440
Hard Spring	320	363	684	182	217	399	285
Soft Red	27	317	344	150	154	304	40
White	68	259	327	55	196	251	76
Durum	86	106	193	49	83	132	61
All classes	924	2,134	3,060	783	1,375	2,158	902
1980/81:							
Hard Winter	440	1,181	1,621	379	701	1,080	541
Hard Spring	285	312	598	153	188	341	257
Soft Red	40	435	475	138	299	437	38
White	76	338	414	54	267	321	93
Durum	61	108	171	52	59	111	60
All classes	902	2,374	3,279	776	1,514	2,290	989
1981/82:							
Hard Winter	541	1,117	1,658	364	755	1,119	539
Hard Spring	257	468	726	172	206	378	348
Soft Red	38	676	714	194	460	654	60
White	93	352	445	66	270	336	109
Durum	60	186	248	58	82	140	108
All classes	989	2,799	3,791	854	1,773	2,627	1,164
1982/83: 3/							
Hard Winter	539	1,255	1,794	384	690	1,074	720
Hard Spring	348	500	852	174	240	414	438
Soft Red	60	610	670	243	340	583	87
White	109	296	405	56	200	256	149
Durum	108	148	259	48	55	103	156
All classes	1,164	2,809	3,980	905	1,525	2,430	1,550

1/Data, except production, are approximations. Imports and exports include flour and products in wheat equivalent. 2/Total supply includes imports. 3/Estimated.

Table 3.--Wheat: marketing year supply and disappearance, specified periods 1979-83*

Year and period	Supply				Ending stocks		
	Beginning stocks	Production	Imports 1/	Total	Gov't owned	Privately owned 2/	Total

- - -Million bushels- - -

Year and period	Beginning stocks	Production	Imports 1/	Total	Gov't owned	Privately owned 2/	Total
1979/80							
June-Sept.	924.1	2,134.1	0.7	3,058.9	49.9	2,220.9	2,270.8
Oct.-Dec.	2,270.8	---	0.5	2,271.3	49.6	1,666.6	1,716.2
Jan.-Mar.	1,716.2	---	0.5	1,716.7	63.3	1,161.8	1,225.1
Apr.-May	1,225.1	---	0.4	1,225.5	141.7	760.3	902.0
Mkt. year	924.1	2,134.1	2.1	3,060.3	141.7	760.3	902.0
1980/81							
June-Sept.	902.0	2,374.3	0.8	3,277.1	202.1	2,270.2	2,472.3
Oct.-Dec.	2,472.3	---	0.6	2,472.9	203.5	1,699.7	1,903.2
Jan.-Mar.	1,903.2	---	0.7	1,903.9	203.2	1,125.4	1,328.6
Apr.-May	1,328.6	---	0.4	1,329.1	199.7	789.1	988.8
Mkt. year	902.0	2,374.3	2.5	3,278.8	199.7	789.1	988.8
1981/82							
June-Sept.	988.8	2,798.7	0.7	3,788.2	191.3	2,543.9	2,735.2
Oct.-Dec.	2,735.2	---	0.8	2,736.0	188.7	1,989.3	2,178.0
Jan.-Mar.	2,178.0	---	0.8	2,178.8	189.1	1,368.0	1,557.1
Apr.-May	1,557.1	---	0.5	1,557.6	190.3	973.6	1,163.9
Mkt. year	988.8	2,798.7	2.8	3,790.3	190.3	973.6	1,163.9
1982/83 4/							
June-Sept.	1,163.9	2,808.7	1.2	3,973.8	190.6	2,796.5	2,987.1
Oct.-Dec.	2,987.1	---	3.0	2,990.1	185.4	2,335.1	2,520.5
Jan.-Mar.	2,520.5	---	2.7	2,523.2	185.2	1,683.7	1,868.9
Apr.-May	1,868.9						
Mkt. year							

Year and period	Disappearance					
	Domestic use				Exports 1/	Total disappearance
	Food	Seed	Feed 3/	Total		

- - -Million bushels- - -

Year and period	Food	Seed	Feed 3/	Total	Exports 1/	Total disappearance
1979/80						
June-Sept.	198.5	33.0	45.6	277.1	511.0	788.1
Oct.-Dec.	157.9	37.0	-27.7	167.2	387.9	555.1
Jan.-Mar.	145.1	1.0	62.8	208.9	282.7	491.6
Apr.-May	94.6	30.0	5.3	129.9	193.6	323.5
Mkt. year	596.1	101.0	86.0	783.1	1,375.2	2,158.3
1980/81						
June-Sept.	197.2	38.0	51.2	286.4	518.4	804.8
Oct.-Dec.	167.1	44.0	-12.8	198.3	371.4	569.7
Jan.-Mar.	150.1	1.0	23.7	174.8	400.4	575.2
Apr.-May	96.1	31.0	-10.4	116.7	223.6	340.3
Mkt. year	610.5	114.0	51.7	776.2	1,513.8	2,290.0
1981/82						
June-Sept.	202.5	37.0	191.7	431.2	621.8	1,053.0
Oct.-Dec.	158.9	46.0	-74.6	130.3	427.4	558.0
Jan.-Mar.	151.7	1.0	28.0	180.7	441.0	621.7
Apr.-May	87.3	28.0	-4.0	111.3	282.4	393.7
Mkt. year	600.4	112.0	141.1	853.5	1,772.6	2,626.4
1982/83 4/						
June-Sept.	206.4	37.0	197.6	441.0	545.7	986.7
Oct.-Dec.	161.8	41.0	-25.8	177.0	292.6	469.6
Jan.-Mar.	151.0	1.0	53.0	205.0	449.3	654.3
Apr.-May						
Mkt. year						

1/ Imports and exports include flour and other products expressed in wheat equivalent. 2/ Includes outstanding and reserve loans. 3/ Residual; approximates feed use and includes negligible quantities used for alcoholic beverages. 4/ Preliminary.

* Totals may not add due to rounding.

Table 3A.--Wheat flour: supply and disappearance, United States, 1968-82

Calendar year	Wheat ground	Millfeed production	Flour production 1/	Flour and product imports 2/	Total supply
	1,000 bu.	1,000 tons	- - - -1,000 cwt- - - -		
1968	569,649	4,511	254,310	233	254,543
1969	567,956	4,458	254,194	274	254,468
1970	563,714	4,409	253,094	325	253,419
1971	555,092	4,279	249,810	341	250,151
1972	557,801	4,303	250,441	477	250,918
1973	567,287	4,395	254,661	550	255,211
1974	562,962	4,483	251,097	665	251,762
1975	582,675	4,701	258,985	621	259,606
1976	618,284	4,920	275,077	604	275,681
1977	618,125	4,787	275,784	604	276,388
1978	621,321	4,860	277,950	773	278,723
1979	636,375	4,945	284,051	823	284,874
1980	628,499	4,867	282,655	904	283,559
1981	634,381	5,044	283,966	1,159	285,125
1982 3/	640,158	5,136	284,965	1,501	286,466

Calendar year	Exports		Domestic disappearance	Total Population July 1	Per capita disappearance
	Flour	Products 2/			
	- - - - - 1,000 cwt - - - - -			Millions	Pounds
1968	28,068	13	226,462	200.7	113
1969	26,333	16	228,119	202.7	113
1970	26,054	14	227,351	205.1	111
1971	20,685	15	229,451	207.7	110
1972	20,335	19	230,564	209.9	110
1973	16,107	26	239,078	211.9	113
1974	14,453	33	237,276	213.9	111
1975	12,364	22	247,220	216.0	114
1976	16,064	44	259,573	218.0	119
1977	22,053	37	254,298	220.2	115
1978	22,170	43	256,510	222.6	115
1979	20,927	86	263,861	225.1	117
1980	17,378	54	266,127	227.7	117
1981	18,655	84	266,386	229.8	116
1982 3/	21,784	154	264,528	232.1	114

1/ Commercial production of wheat flour, whole wheat, industrial and durum flour and farina
reported by Bureau of Census. Production prior to 1970 includes estimate for non-commercial
wheat milled. 2/ Imports and exports of macaroni products (flour equivalent).
3/ Preliminary. Note: Per capita disappearance is based upon the indicated population
estimate. The estimates for 1970-81 have been adjusted to make them consistent with the 1980
census.

Table 4.--Wheat, flour and wheat products, United States exports by months, 1980-83*

1,000 bushels

1980/81					
June	96,193	4,230	912	101,335	101,335
July	123,598	2,082	1,222	126,902	228,237
August	141,415	5,057	711	147,183	375,420
September	137,325	3,774	1,849	142,949	518,369
October	116,948	2,785	1,284	121,017	639,386
November	112,199	2,165	1,005	115,369	754,755
December	132,048	1,739	1,230	135,017	889,772
January	129,981	2,658	890	133,529	1,023,301
February	124,397	5,217	1,010	130,624	1,153,925
March	128,770	6,353	1,114	136,238	1,290,163
April	127,652	7,347	4,433	139,432	1,429,596
May	78,030	4,803	1,406	84,239	1,513,835
Mkt. year	1,448,558	48,209	17,068	1,513,835	
1981/82					
June	124,521	5,794	1,827	132,142	132,142
July	138,168	2,779	1,150	142,097	274,239
August	145,428	3/ 3,438	1,009	3/ 149,875	424,114
September	194,148	2,496	1,037	197,681	621,795
October	156,993	3/ 668	1,171	3/ 158,832	780,627
November	127,495	3/ 411	1,406	3/ 129,312	909,939
December	137,757	3/ 902	572	3/ 139,231	1,049,170
January	124,163	1,767	1,211	127,141	1,176,311
February	138,719	8,068	1,875	148,662	1,324,973
March	159,078	5,775	351	165,204	1,490,177
April	148,181	8,838	2,246	159,265	1,649,442
May	116,496	5,983	692	123,171	1,772,613
Mkt. year	1,711,147	46,919	14,547	1,772,613	
1982/83					
June	156,914	4,587	971	162,472	162,472
July	117,914	1,393	476	119,783	282,255
August	124,336	3,499	1,073	128,908	411,164
September	130,992	2,527	984	134,503	545,667
October	98,520	3,909	3/ 529	3/ 102,957	648,624
November	94,638	3/ 2,483	3/ 2,604	3/ 99,726	748,350
December	88,457	3/ 999	3/ 472	3/ 89,928	838,278
January	143,140	6,389	2,039	151,568	989,846
February	146,594	9,999	709	157,302	1,147,148
March	131,134	7,765	1,536	140,435	1,287,583
April					
May					
Mkt. year					

1/ Includes meal and groats. 2/ Includes macaroni and bulgar. 3/ Revised by Census.

* Totals may not add due to rounding.

Source: Bureau of the Census.

Table 5.--Wheat: price support loan status on specified dates, 1976-82 crops

Crop of	Total loans	Put in reserve	Repaid		Delivered to CCC	Outstanding	
			Loans	Reserve		Loans	Reserve

Million bushels

As of June 1, 1982

Crop of	Total loans	Put in reserve	Loans	Reserve	Delivered to CCC	Loans	Reserve
1976	498.8	216.1	234.7	158.3	48.0	--	57.8
1977	590.8	195.0	393.6	140.0	2.2	--	55.0
1978	255.1	24.1	231.0	4.5	--	--	19.6
1979	180.5	40.0	140.5	5.7	--	--	34.3
1980	329.4	206.1	123.0	3.2	--	0.3	202.9
1981	445.8	191.1	141.7	0.3	1.3	111.7	190.8
Total	***	***	***	***	1/190.3	112.0	560.4

As of October 1, 1982

Crop of	Total loans	Put in reserve	Loans	Reserve	Delivered to CCC	Loans	Reserve
1976	498.8	216.1	234.7	158.7	48.0	--	57.4
1977	590.8	195.0	393.6	140.2	2.2	--	54.8
1978	255.1	24.1	231.0	4.5	--	--	19.6
1979	180.5	40.0	140.5	5.8	--	--	34.2
1980	329.4	206.2	123.0	3.6	--	0.2	202.6
1981	445.8	217.6	175.0	0.6	7.3	45.9	217.0
1982	335.2	283.4	0.8	---	--	51.0	283.4
Total	***	***	***	***	1/190.6	97.1	869.0

As of January 1, 1983

Crop of	Total loans	Put in reserve	Loans	Reserve	Delivered to CCC	Loans	Reserve
1976	498.8	216.1	234.7	159.7	48.0	--	5 .4
1977	590.8	195.0	393.6	140.3	2.2	--	5 .7
1978	255.1	24.0	231.1	4.7	--	--	16.3
1979	180.5	40.0	140.5	5.9	--	--	39.1
1980	329.4	206.2	123.0	3.8	--	0.2	202.4
1981	445.8	229.4	177.2	0.6	10.9	28.3	228.8
1982	501.1	422.4	4.5	0.3	--	74.2	422.1
Total	***	***	***	***	1/185.4	102.7	1,017.8

As of April 1, 1983

Crop of	Total loans	Put in reserve	Loans	Reserve	Delivered to CCC	Loans	Reserve
1976	498.8	216.1	234.7	194.8	48.0	--	21.3
1977	590.8	195.0	393.6	159.4	2.2	--	35.6
1978	255.1	23.9	231.2	7.4	--	--	16.5
1979	180.5	39.7	140.8	10.7	--	--	29.0
1980	329.4	205.2	123.1	4.1	--	1.1	201.1
1981	445.8	237.7	176.1	0.9	13.1	18.9	236.8
1982	629.4	555.3	12.2	0.7	0.1	61.8	554.6
Total	***	***	***	***	1/ 185.2	81.8	1,094.9

1/Includes outstanding CCC-owned stocks from loan forfeitures and open market purchases in March 1980.

Source: Agricultural Stabilization and Conservation Service loan activity reports.

Table 6.--White pan bread: estimated price and marketing spreads of ingredients per 1-pound loaf and per cwt of flour, Oct.-Dec. 1981-1982*

Item 1/	Oct.-Dec. 1981		Oct.-Dec. 1982	
	Value per loaf	Value per cwt of flour	Value per loaf	Value per cwt of flour
	Cents	Dollars	Cents	Dollars
Retail price (BLS)	52.30	84.09	53.50	86.02
Price spreads				
Wholesale-to-retail 2/	8.77	14.11	9.01	14.49
Baking 3/	33.71	54.20	35.26	56.69
Flour milling	1.06	1.71	1.03	1.65
Other spreads				
Wheat, farm-to-flour mill	.84	1.35	1.05	1.68
Other farm ingredients 4/	.90	1.45	.80	1.29
Flour, flour mill-to-baker	.62	1.00	.53	.86
Nonfarm ingredients 5/	1.03	1.66	1.06	1.71
Total farm-retail price spread	46.93	75.46	48.74	78.36
Farm value of ingredients				
Wheat	4.69	7.54	4.19	6.73
Other farm ingredients	.68	1.08	.58	.93
Total farm value	5.36	8.63	4.76	7.66
Cost of farm ingredients				
Flour				
F.o.b. bakery	7.21	11.06	6.79	10.92
F.o.b. flour mill	6.59	10.60	6.26	10.07
Wheat 6/				
F.o.b. flour mill	5.53	8.89	5.23	8.42
Farm value	4.69	7.54	4.19	6.73
Other farm ingredients:				
F.o.b. bakery	1.57	2.53	1.38	2.21
Farm value	.68	1.08	.58	.93

	Dollars per cwt	
Prices of flour and millfeeds		
Flour f.o.b. bakery	11.60	10.92
Flour f.o.b. flour mill	10.60	10.07
Millfeeds, f.o.b. flour mill	4.69	4.41

	Dollars per bushel	
Prices of wheat		
Wheat, f.o.b. flour mill	4.50	4.27
Farm value	3.82	3.42

1/ Price spreads may not add because of independent rounding. 2/ Difference between retail and wholesale price of bread. 3/ Difference between wholesale price and cost of bread ingredients, f.o.b. bakery. 4/ Includes processing, transportation, and merchandising for lard, soybean oil, HFCS, corn sirup, and soy-whey blend. Difference between estimated cost to baker and estimated farm value. 5/ Estimated cost to baker of yeast, yeast food, salt, and other nonfarm ingredients. 6/ Price adjusted for value of millfeeds.

* Spreads are developed by L.D. Schnake (Economist) and Karen Stuart, ERS, USDA, at the U.S. Grain Marketing Research Laboratory, Manhattan, Kansas 66502, (913) 539-9141.

Table 7.--Wheat and flour: price relationships at milling centers, annual and by periods, 1978-83

Year and period	At Kansas City					At Minneapolis				
	Cost of wheat to produce 100 lb. of flour 1/	Wholesale price of				Cost of wheat to produce 100 lb. of flour 1/	Wholesale price of			
		Bakery flour per 100 lb. 2/	Byproducts obtained 100 lb. flour 3/	Total products			Bakery flour per 100 lb. 2/	Byproducts obtained 100 lb. flour 3/	Total products	
				Actual	Over cost of wheat				Actual	Over cost of wheat
	Dollars									
1978/79										
June-Sept.	7.29	7.49	1.27	8.76	1.47	7.27	8.03	1.16	9.19	1.92
Oct.-Dec.	7.83	7.77	1.67	9.44	1.61	7.78	8.15	1.48	9.63	1.85
Jan.-Mar.	7.98	7.84	1.61	9.45	1.47	7.74	8.05	1.44	9.49	1.75
Apr.-May	8.31	8.46	1.35	9.81	1.50	8.26	8.65	1.29	9.94	1.68
Mkt. year	7.85	7.89	1.47	9.36	1.51	7.76	8.22	1.34	9.56	1.80
1979/80										
June-Sept.	9.87	9.91	1.70	11.61	1.74	9.88	10.22	1.61	11.83	1.95
Oct.-Dec.	10.50	10.39	1.85	12.24	1.74	9.99	10.57	1.63	12.20	2.21
Jan.-Mar.	9.79	10.02	1.77	11.79	2.00	9.46	10.20	1.45	11.65	2.19
Apr.-May	9.24	9.75	1.50	11.25	2.01	9.61	10.04	1.36	11.40	1.79
Mkt. year	9.85	10.02	1.70	11.72	1.87	9.73	10.26	1.51	11.77	2.04
1980/81										
June-Sept.	9.81	10.11	1.81	11.92	2.11	10.46	10.83	1.63	12.46	2.00
Oct.-Dec.	10.80	10.54	2.38	12.92	2.12	11.29	11.04	2.05	13.09	1.80
Jan.-Mar.	10.31	10.44	1.95	12.39	2.08	10.98	11.05	1.67	12.72	1.74
Apr.-May	10.27	10.42	1.81	12.23	1.96	11.08	11.09	1.76	12.85	1.77
Mkt. year	10.30	10.38	1.99	12.37	2.07	10.95	11.00	1.78	12.78	1.83
1981/82										
June-Sept.	9.69	10.33	1.55	11.88	2.19	10.08	10.82	1.49	12.31	2.23
Oct.-Dec.	9.93	10.13	1.79	11.92	1.99	9.84	10.52	1.43	11.95	2.11
Jan.-Mar.	9.85	10.66	1.41	12.07	2.22	9.63	10.82	1.23	12.05	2.42
Apr.-May	9.76	10.38	1.52	11.90	2.14	9.64	10.54	1.48	12.02	2.38
Mkt. year	9.81	10.37	1.57	11.94	2.13	9.80	10.67	1.41	12.08	2.28
1982/83 4/										
June-Sept.	9.24	10.14	1.39	11.53	2.29	9.31	10.43	1.25	11.68	2.37
Oct.-Dec.	9.22	10.06	1.58	11.64	2.42	9.22	10.43	1.29	11.72	2.50
Jan.-Mar.	9.60	10.40	1.47	11.87	2.27	9.15	10.41	1.10	11.51	2.36
Apr.-May										
Mkt. year										

1/Based on 73 percent extraction rate, cost of 2.28 bushels: At Kansas City, No. 1 Hd. Winter, 13 percent protein, and at Minneapolis, simple average of No. 1 Dark Northern Spring, 13 and 15 percent protein. 2/Quoted as 95 percent patent at Kansas City and standard patent at Minneapolis, bulk basis. 3/Assumed 50-50 millfeed distribution between bran and shorts or middlings, bulk basis. 4/Preliminary.

Source: Compiled from reports of Agricultural Marketing Service and Department of Labor.

Table 8.--Wheat: farm price for leading classes and major feed grains in region, 1979-83 1/

Commodity and year	June	July	Aug.	Sept.	Oct.	Nov.	Dec.	Jan.	Feb.	Mar.	Apr.	May	Simple average	Loan rate
					All prices for 60 pounds									
				Central and So. Plains (Hard Winter) 2/										
Wheat:														
1979/80	3.63	3.81	3.72	3.82	3.86	3.93	3.89	3.81	3.73	3.51	3.36	3.48	.71	2.43
1980/81	3.49	3.63	3.75	3.86	4.10	4.19	4.01	4.08	3.99	3.83	3.88	3.75	.88	2.94
1981/82	3.77	3.72	3.68	3.69	3.76	3.87	3.82	3.78	3.74	3.71	3.72	3.66	3.74	3.13
1982/83	3.49	3.37	3.34	3.38	3.36	3.43	3.49	3.51	3.51	3.61				3.36
Sorghum:														
1979/80	2.55	2.68	2.51	2.48	2.45	2.45	2.41	2.43	2.44	2.47	2.40	2.45	2.48	2.12
1980/81	2.58	2.94	3.06	3.18	3.31	3.33	3.34	3.33	3.28	3.14	3.18	3.12	3.15	2.27
1981/82	3.03	2.96	2.65	2.37	2.34	2.36	2.39	2.44	2.42	2.43	2.47	2.61	2.54	2.42
1982/83	2.60	2.57	2.49	2.44	2.26	2.34	2.41	2.48	2.68	2.84				2.57
				Cornbelt (Soft Red Winter) 3/										
Wheat:														
1979/80	3.85	4.01	3.86	3.93	4.00	3.87	3.99	4.03	4.11	3.82	3.59	3.62	.89	2.48
1980/81	3.58	3.82	4.02	4.19	4.41	4.59	4.50	4.50	4.28	4.03	4.00	3.59	.13	3.00
1981/82	3.35	3.46	3.36	3.45	3.56	3.68	3.70	3.71	3.40	3.36	3.42	3.23	3.47	3.20
1982/83	3.18	3.08	2.98	2.89	2.75	3.02	3.13	3.18	3.20	3.30				3.56
Corn:														
1979/80	2.78	3.02	2.88	2.81	2.59	2.48	2.71	2.66	2.65	2.63	2.60	2.68	2.71	2.31
1980/81	2.76	3.06	3.28	3.36	3.28	3.46	3.53	3.54	3.58	3.58	3.57	3.56	3.38	2.46
1981/82	3.47	3.44	3.11	2.76	2.64	2.52	2.54	2.74	2.63	2.66	2.77	2.86	2.85	2.62
1982/83	2.82	2.76	2.57	2.30	2.09	2.29	2.48	2.57	2.77	2.96				2.78
				Northern Plains (Spring and Durum) 4/										
Other spring														
1979/80	3.50	3.69	3.59	3.65	3.74	3.64	3.57	3.48	3.55	3.53	3.60	3.73	3.61	2.51
1980/81	3.82	4.04	3.95	3.96	4.15	4.24	4.18	4.23	4.19	4.15	4.25	4.24	4.12	3.02
1981/82	4.12	3.93	3.70	3.62	3.66	3.74	3.63	3.69	3.67	3.61	3.73	3.69	3.73	3.21
1982/83	3.62	3.59	3.46	3.45	3.44	3.51	3.47	3.45	3.41	3.61				3.57
Durum:														
1979/80	N	O	T		A	V	A	I	L	A	B	L	E	2.51
1980/81														3.02
1981/82	4.52	3.91	3.52	3.41	3.51	3.55	3.47	3.60	3.67	3.52	3.54	3.52	3.64	3.21
1982/83	3.50	3.36	3.10	3.09	3.19	3.25	3.16	3.40	3.22	3.47				3.57
				Pacific Northwest (White) 5/										
Wheat:														
1979/80	3.98	3.93	4.12	4.03	3.91	3.89	3.73	3.68	3.80	3.71	3.66	3.56	3.83	2.57
1980/81	3.53	3.71	3.67	3.80	4.03	4.12	4.08	4.05	4.06	4.11	4.02	4.08	3.94	3.08
1981/82	3.97	3.69	3.78	3.80	3.94	3.96	3.98	3.91	3.75	3.68	3.72	3.71	3.82	3.29
1982/83	3.71	3.62	3.74	3.76	3.86	3.91	3.98	4.07	4.15	4.18				3.65
Barley:														
1979/80	2.69	3.08	3.00	3.09	3.07	3.34	3.10	3.10	3.10	3.18	3.21	3.12	3.09	2.26
1980/81	3.16	3.34	3.32	3.35	3.70	3.80	3.99	4.07	4.15	4.07	3.95	3.99	3.74	2.40
1981/82	3.72	3.39	3.19	3.10	3.08	3.34	3.20	3.24	3.21	3.39	3.41	3.45	3.31	2.55
1982/83	3.25	3.02	3.11	2.73	2.58	2.70	2.94	2.83	2.88	2.82				2.71
				U.S. average										
Wheat:														
1979/80	3.72	3.89	3.74	3.87	3.98	3.94	3.81	3.74	3.78	3.64	3.58	3.69	6/3.78	2.50
1980/81	3.69	3.81	3.94	3.99	4.19	4.32	4.22	4.21	4.17	4.09	4.07	3.95	6/3.91	3.00
1981/82	3.70	3.62	3.62	3.65	3.77	3.85	3.80	3.78	3.70	3.67	3.68	3.64	6/3.65	3.20
1982/83	3.39	3.26	3.34	3.38	3.43	3.48	3.51	3.57	3.57	3.66			6/3.53	3.55

1/To adjust price to relative feed value multiply: corn 1.00; wheat 1.05; barley .90; sorghum .95; reported in Consumption of Feed by Livestock, Report No. 79, ERS, USDA. 2/Kansas, Nebraska, Texas, Oklahoma, and Colorado. 3/Ohio, Indiana, Illinois, and Missouri. 4/North Dakota, South Dakota, and Minnesota. 5/Washington, Oregon, and Idaho. 6/Season average price includes allowance for unredeemed loans and purchases.

Dollars per bushel

Kansas City, No. 1 Hard Red Winter (ordinary protein)

1979/80	4.17	4.34	4.12	4.26	4.39	4.53	4.51	4.33	4.32	4.07	3.90	4.10	4.25
1980/81	4.07	4.21	4.31	4.45	4.70	4.89	4.54	4.60	4.47	4.35	4.48	4.36	4.45
1981/82	4.24	4.25	4.14	4.19	4.31	4.46	4.35	4.33	4.26	4.25	4.28	4.22	4.27
1982/83	4.06	3.74	3.70	3.75	3.61	3.86	3.98	4.00	4.08	4.18			

13% protein

1979/80	4.22	4.42	4.28	4.39	4.55	4.67	4.60	4.40	4.35	4.14	3.96	4.14	4.34
1980/81	4.12	4.25	4.34	4.49	4.70	4.91	4.60	4.67	4.50	4.40	4.57	4.44	4.50
1981/82	4.36	4.26	4.16	4.22	4.29	4.44	4.33	4.35	4.32	4.29	4.32	4.24	4.30
1982/83	4.15	4.12	4.00	3.94	3.80	4.09	4.24	4.19	4.17	4.27			

Chicago, No. 2 Soft Red Winter

1979/80	4.36	4.39	4.23	4.28	4.30	4.13	4.26	4.36	4.39	4.18	3.96	4.04	4.24
1980/81	3.96	4.17	4.21	4.38	4.70	4.92	4.54	4.57	4.34	4.15	4.18	3.80	4.33
1981/82	3.60	3.70	3.70	3.87	3.97	4.08	3.86	3.77	3.57	3.59	3.70	3.43	3.74
1982/83	3.31	3.36	3.35	3.18	2.98	3.33	3.23	3.32	3.40	3.36			

St. Louis, No. 2 Soft Red Winter

1979/80	4.08	4.18	4.04	4.08	4.02	4.10	4.28	4.26	4.32	4.11	3.80	3.93	4.10
1980/81	3.73	4.10	4.19	4.42	4.78	4.96	4.78	4.80	4.57	4.32	4.36	3.67	4.39
1981/82	3.41	3.54	3.56	3.67	3.74	4.05	3.90	3.76	3.60	3.61	3.72	3.31	3.66
1982/83	3.25	3.27	3.14	3.06	3.06	3.38	3.28	3.33	3.41	3.43			

Toledo, No. 2 Soft Red Winter

1979/80	4.17	4.37	4.22	4.28	4.29	4.21	4.28	4.21	4.32	4.08	3.80	3.90	4.18
1980/81	3.84	4.14	4.16	4.38	4.82	5.02	4.65	4.70	4.47	4.16	4.16	3.76	4.36
1981/82	3.55	3.63	3.71	3.83	3.98	4.08	3.85	3.71	3.47	3.46	3.63	3.45	3.70
1982/83	3.35	3.36	3.28	3.09	2.84	3.19	3.23	3.28	3.32	3.29			

Toledo, No. 2 Soft White

1979/80	4.08	4.31	4.15	4.17	4.12	4.20	4.18	4.10	4.14	3.90	3.63	3.74	4.06
1980/81	3.71	4.05	4.15	4.31	--	--	4.44	4.49	4.21	3.87	3.87	3.62	4.07
1981/82	3.43	3.62	3.77	3.91	3.99	4.10	3.82	3.68	3.49	3.47	3.61	3.45	3.70
1982/83	3.35	3.49	3.42	3.22	2.92	3.22	3.29	3.25	3.39	3.43			

Portland, No. 1 Soft White

1979/80	4.46	4.67	4.45	4.31	4.13	4.16	4.10	4.10	4.26	4.13	4.02	3.91	4.22
1980/81	3.92	4.15	4.06	4.23	4.48	4.68	4.40	4.52	4.52	4.41	4.51	4.41	4.36
1981/82	4.26	4.27	4.25	4.21	4.38	4.42	4.00	4.12	4.09	4.02	4.14	4.24	4.20
1982/83	4.18	4.13	4.16	4.29	4.29	4.44	4.45	4.52	4.59	4.68			

Minneapolis, No. 1 Dark No. Spring (ordinary protein)

1979/80	4.23	4.31	4.10	4.18	4.31	4.27	4.18	4.06	4.13	4.04	3.94	4.21	4.16
1980/81	4.19	4.54	4.22	4.17	4.62	4.78	4.62	4.65	4.53	4.32	4.41	4.44	4.46
1981/82	4.29	4.18	4.03	4.07	4.22	4.29	4.15	4.21	4.17	4.10	4.21	4.16	4.17
1982/83	4.08	4.08	3.78	3.79	3.78	3.85	3.76	3.80	3.82	4.01			

14% protein

1979/80	4.32	4.42	4.19	4.29	4.45	4.29	4.17	4.07	4.08	4.02	3.96	4.31	4.21
1980/81	4.33	4.69	4.55	4.56	4.82	4.95	4.77	4.81	4.78	4.67	4.80	4.77	4.71
1981/82	4.56	4.50	4.25	4.23	4.29	4.38	4.22	4.28	4.21	4.16	4.25	4.20	4.29
1982/83	4.13	4.16	3.96	4.02	4.00	4.08	3.96	3.93	3.92	4.08			

Hard Amber Durum, No. 1 (medium)

1979/80	4.75	4.99	4.88	5.27	5.80	5.38	4.99	4.93	5.05	4.98	4.89	5.21	5.09
1980/81	5.79	7.12	7.19	7.26	7.34	7.22	6.90	7.07	7.02	6.66	6.10	6.04	6.81
1981/82	4.86	4.91	4.75	4.56	4.60	4.58	4.51	4.59	4.57	4.45	4.45	4.49	4.61
1982/83	4.38	4.26	4.07	4.02	4.11	4.17	4.07	4.06	4.12	4.28			

Source: Grain Market News, Agricultural Marketing Service.

Table 10.--Wheat: export prices by months, at selected ports, 1979-83

Dollars per metric ton

Gulf: No. 1 Hard Red Winter, ordinary protein

Year													
1979/80	168	175	169	174	178	178	180	176	173	164	156	161	171
1980/81	158	169	171	180	188	195	182	187	182	175	180	172	178
1981/82	169	168	170	171	169	179	175	173	171	169	170	168	171
1982/83	156	152	153	153	147	155	160	165	165	166			

Gulf: No. 1 Soft Red Winter

Year													
1979/80	164	169	163	165	163	164	172	170	168	162	153	154	164
1980/81	146	163	165	176	187	193	180	187	176	168	172	143	171
1981/82	133	136	140	147	150	157	151	148	142	144	149	128	144
1982/83	126	128	122	119	113	129	128	131	133	133			

Portland: No. 2 Western White

Year													
1979/80	171	178	167	163	160	157	155	157	162	157	155	148	161
1980/81	147	158	157	162	172	180	170	174	173	166	166	165	166
1981/82	159	159	161	161	165	166	152	155	152	152	155	157	158
1982/83	156	153	158	162	161	167	168	169	172	174			

Duluth: No. 2 Northern Spring, 14% protein

Year													
1979/80	163	166	1/	1/	167	158	1/	1/	1/	1/	146	158	159
1980/81	158	174	168	170	177	180	1/	1/	1/	1/	176	175	172
1981/82	170	164	159	156	158	161	1/	1/	1/	1/	164	154	161
1982/83	151	152	146	148	147	149	1/	1/	1/	1/			

1/No price quotes available.

Source: Grain Market News, Agricultural Marketing Service.

Table 11.--Wheat: rotterdam, c.i.f., quotations by months, 1979-83 1/

Dollars per metric ton

United States No. 2 Hard Winter, 13.5%

Year													
1979/80	193	204	200	205	209	212	212	200	200	197	NQ	NQ	203
1980/81	203	204	209	214	224	233	235	233	225	212	211	206	217
1981/82	203	204	201	200	200	212	206	200	199	198	206	204	203
1982/83	176	176	2/	2/	2/	2/	2/	2/	2/	2/			

United States Dark Northern Spring, 14%

Year													
1979/80	192	202	194	199	205	204	205	206	205	196	188	199	200
1980/81	197	194	189	212	216	226	235	245	240	209	210	207	215
1981/82	197	194	189	190	193	196	190	204	204	195	190	184	194
1982/83	178	178	174	174	171	177	183	185	178	172			

1/Hamburg Mercantile Exchange prices for Rotterdam. 2/No price quotes available.

Source: World Grain Situation, Foreign Agricultural Service.

Table 12.--Wheat and wheat flour: world trade, production, stocks, and utilization, July-June 1980-83

Million metric tons

Exports:				
Canada	17.0	17.8	21.0	21.5
Australia	10.6	11.0	7.5	11.0
Argentina	3.9	4.3	8.5	6.5
EC-10	14.7	15.5	15.5	15.5
USSR	0.5	0.5	0.5	0.5
All others	5.6	4.1	5.7	4.4
Total non-U.S.	52.3	53.1	58.7	59.4
USA 1/	41.9	49.1	41.5	38.0
World total	94.2	102.2	100.2	97.4
Imports:				
EC-10	4.5	4.7	3.7	4.0
USSR	16.0	19.5	21.0	19.0
Japan	5.8	5.6	5.6	5.5
E. Europe	5.9	6.4	4.3	4.0
China	13.8	13.2	13.0	12.0
All others	48.2	52.9	52.7	52.9
World total	94.2	102.2	100.2	97.4
Production: 2/				
Canada	19.2	24.8	27.6	26.5
Australia	10.9	16.3	8.7	17.0
Argentina	7.8	8.1	14.5	11.5
EC-10	55.1	54.4	59.6	60.7
USSR 3/	98.2	80.0	86.0	90.0
E. Europe	34.5	30.5	33.9	33.1
China	55.2	59.6	68.4	71.0
India	31.8	36.3	37.8	39.5
All other foreign	64.3	62.3	66.3	64.5
USA	64.6	76.2	76.4	64.0
World total	441.5	448.6	479.3	477.8
Utilization: 4/				
USA	21.1	23.2	24.6	26.1
USSR 3/	116.7	99.0	106.5	99.5
China	69.0	72.8	81.4	83.0
All other foreign	239.8	245.7	253.1	253.7
World total	446.6	440.8	465.6	462.4
Stocks, ending: 5/	75.3	83.1	96.7	112.2

1/Includes transshipments through Canadian ports; excludes products other than flour. 2/Production data include all harvests occurring within the July-June year shown, except that small grain crops from the early harvesting Northern Hemisphere areas are moved forward; i.e., the May 1980 harvests in areas such as India, North Africa, and Southern United States are actually included in 1980/81 accounting period, which begins July 1, 1980. 3/"Bunker weight" basis: not discounted for excess moisture and foreign material. 4/Utilization data are based on an aggregate of differing local marketing years. For countries for which stock data are not available (excluding the USSR), utilization estimates represent apparent utilization, i.e., they are inclusive of annual stock level adjustments. 5/Stocks data are based on an aggregate of differing local marketing years and should not be construed as representing world stock levels at a fixed point in time. Stocks data are not available for all countries and exclude those such as China and part of Eastern Europe; the world stock levels have been adjusted for estimated year-to-year changes in USSR grain stocks, but do not purport to include the entire absolute level of USSR stocks.

Source: Foreign Agricultural Service. World Grain Situation.

Table 13.--Rye: supply, disappearance, area, and prices, marketing years 1978-82*

	Million bushels				
Supply					
Beginning stocks, June 1	4.0	9.0	12.2	4.1	3.1
Production	24.1	22.4	16.5	18.8	20.8
Imports	0.1	1/	1/	0.4	2.6
Total	28.2	31.4	28.7	23.4	26.5
Domestic disappearance					
Food	3.7	3.5	3.5	3.5	3.4
Industry	2.4	2.1	2.1	2.2	2.4
Seed	4.6	4.0	4.2	4.2	4.2
Feed 2/	8.1	7.1	7.3	8.9	9.0
Total	18.8	16.7	17.1	18.8	19.0
Exports	0.4	2.4	7.5	1.5	0.2
Total disappearance	19.2	19.2	24.6	20.3	19.2
Ending stocks, May 31	9.0	12.2	4.1	3.1	7.3
	Million acres				
Area					
Planted	2.9	2.9	2.5	2.6	2.6
Harvested	0.9	0.9	0.7	0.7	0.7
	Bushels per acre				
Yield per harvested acre	26.0	25.8	24.4	26.7	29.1
	Dollars per bushel				
Prices					
Received by farmers	1.99	2.06	2.63	2.99	2.41
Minneapolis No. 2	2.44	2.47	3.35	3.80	
Loan rate	1.70	1.79	1.91	2.04	2.17

1/ Less than 50,000 bushels. 2/ Residual, approximates total feed use.

* Totals may not add due to rounding.

Table 14.--Rye: marketing year supply and disappearance, specified periods, 1980-83

Year and period	Supply				
	Beginning stocks	Production	Imports	Total supply	Ending stocks

- - -1,000 bushels- - -

Year and period	Beginning stocks	Production	Imports	Total supply	Ending stocks
1980/81					
June-Sept.	12,192	16,483	5	28,680	18,510
Oct.-Dec.	18,510	---	1	18,511	9,346
Jan.-Mar.	9,346	---	4	9,350	6,868
Apr.-May	6,858	---	1/	6,868	4,145
Mkt. year	12,192	16,483	TO	28,685	4,145
1981/82					
June-Sept.	4,145	18,822	33	23,000	14,551
Oct.-Dec.	14,551	---	6	14,557	7,882
Jan.-Mar.	7,882	---	72	7,954	5,785
Apr.-May	5,785	---	321	6,106	3,095
Mkt. year	4,145	18,822	432	23,399	3,095
1982/83 2/					
June-Sept.	3,095	20,817	821	24,733	16,460
Oct.-Dec.	16,460	---	1,044	17,504	10,868
Jan.-Mar.	10,868	---	623	11,491	7,961
Apr.-May					
Mkt. year					

Year and period	Disappearance						
	Domestic use					Exports	Total disappearance
	Food	Seed	Industry	Feed 3/	Total		

- - -1,000 bushels- - -

Year and period	Food	Seed	Industry	Feed 3/	Total	Exports	Total disappearance
1980/81							
June-Sept.	1,150	2,075	370	3,364	6,959	3,211	10,170
Oct.-Dec.	960	1,868	486	2,726	6,040	3,125	9,165
Jan.-Mar.	821	207	707	30	1,765	717	2,482
Apr.-May	584	---	487	1,211	2,282	441	2,723
Mkt. year	3,515	4,150	2,050	7,331	17,046	7,494	24,540
1981/82							
June-Sept.	1,170	2,080	419	4,732	8,401	48	8,449
Oct.-Dec.	881	1,872	624	1,939	5,316	1,359	6,675
Jan.-Mar.	885	208	779	187	2,059	110	2,169
Apr.-May	522	---	420	2,057	2,999	12	3,011
Mkt. year	3,458	4,160	2,242	8,915	18,775	1,529	20,304
1982/83 2/							
June-Sept.	1,162	2,120	529	4,369	8,180	93	8,273
Oct.-Dec.	883	1,908	650	3,166	6,607	29	6,636
Jan.-Mar.	770	212	790	1,708	3,480	50	3,530
Apr.-May							
Mkt. year							

1/ Less than 500 bushels. 2/ Preliminary. 3/ Residual; approximates total feed use.

The Answers
Are as Near as
Your Telephone . . .

900-410-FARM

Farmers, ranchers, and other agribusiness professionals agree on one thing:
any good business decision is an "informed"
business decision.

Agline is a telephone information
service providing current economic and statis-
tical news from the U.S. Department of Agriculture.

Agline is available weekly (**Thursday** midnight to Friday
midnight) beginning **April 29, 1983,** currently in the **Central Time
Zone.** The 3-minute summary will cost about **$1.20** on your tele-
phone bill.

Before you make a production or agribusiness decision,
call USDA's **Agline.**

Agline 900-410-FARM

CPSIA information can be obtained
at www.ICGtesting.com
Printed in the USA
BVHW041524231118
533817BV00018B/1150/P

9 781528 096638